101 *Easy* EVERYDAY RECIPES

Breakfast Bruschetta, page 17

White Chocolate–Butterscotch Pretzels, page 103

Sweet-and-Sour Slaw, page 82

Gooseberry Patch
2500 Farmers Dr., #110
Columbus, OH 43235

www.gooseberrypatch.com
1·800·854·6673

Gooseberry Patch *cookbooks*

Easiest Cinnamon-Raisin Rolls, page 21

Hawaiian Asparagus, page 83

Since 1992, we've been publishing our own country cookbooks for every kitchen and for every meal of the day! Each title has hundreds of budget-friendly recipes, using ingredients you already have on hand in your pantry.

In addition, you'll find helpful tips and ideas on every page, along with our hand-drawn artwork and plenty of personality. Their lay-flat binding makes them so easy to use...they're sure to become a fast favorite in your kitchen.

Call us toll-free at

1•800•854•6673

and we'd be delighted to tell you all about our newest titles!

Shop with us online anytime at

www.gooseberrypatch.com

Send us your favorite recipe!

and the memory that makes it special for you!* If we select your recipe for a brand-new **Gooseberry Patch** cookbook, your name will appear right along with it...and you'll receive a FREE copy of the book!

Submit your recipe on our website at
www.gooseberrypatch.com

Or mail to:

Gooseberry Patch • Attn: Cookbook Dept.
2500 Farmers Dr., #110 • Columbus, OH 43235

*Please include the number of servings and all other necessary information!

Have a taste for more?

Visit **www.gooseberrypatch.com** to join our **Circle of Friends**!

- Free recipes, tips and ideas plus a complete cookbook index
- Get special email offers and our monthly E-letter delivered to your inbox
- Find local stores with **Gooseberry Patch** cookbooks, calendars and organizers

Coconut–Orange Breakfast Rolls, page 8

Apple–Stuffed Turkey Breast, page 46

BBQ Beef & Wagon Wheels Salad, page 77

Chocolate–Berry Trifles, page 93

Ripe Tomato Tart, page 70

Sunday Meatball Skillet, page 43

Orange-Filled Napoleons, page 88

CONTENTS

Easy-Breezy Breakfasts 7

Toss-Together Suppers 28

Dinner's in the Oven 48

Sides in a Snap 68

No-Fuss Desserts 88

Peachy Waffle Topping, page 14

Dedication
To those who
delight in making
every meal special!

Appreciation
A heartfelt thanks
to all who sent us
their delicious and
oh-so-simple recipes!

Hug in a Mug Soup, page 37

Egg & Bacon Quesadillas

2 T. butter, divided
4 8-inch flour tortillas
5 eggs, beaten
1/2 c. milk
2 8-oz. pkgs. shredded
   Cheddar cheese
6 to 8 slices bacon, crisply
   cooked and crumbled
Optional: salsa, sour cream

Lightly spread about 1/4 teaspoon butter on one side of each tortilla; set aside. In a bowl, beat eggs and milk until combined. Pour egg mixture into a hot, lightly greased skillet; cook and stir over medium heat until done. Remove scrambled eggs to a dish and keep warm. Melt remaining butter in the skillet and add a tortilla, buttered-side down. Layer with 1/4 of the cheese, 1/2 of the eggs and 1/2 of the bacon. Top with 1/4 of the cheese and a tortilla, buttered-side up. Cook one to 2 minutes on each side, until golden. Repeat with remaining ingredients. Cut each into 4 wedges and serve with salsa and sour cream, if desired. Serves 4.

Joshua Logan
Corpus Christi, TX
My kids raved about these after a sleepover at their Aunt Sherry's house. I like to spice up mine with hot sauce!

Coconut-Orange Breakfast Rolls

12.4-oz. tube refrigerated
  cinnamon rolls with icing
3/4 to 1 c. sweetened flaked
  coconut
1 t. canola oil
1/2 c. orange marmalade
1/4 c. sliced almonds
1/2 to 1 t. almond extract

Separate dough into 8 rolls; set icing
aside. Place coconut in a dish. Roll
each roll in coconut, pressing to make
sure sides are covered. Place rolls,
cinnamon-side up, into a 9" round
cake pan coated with oil. Make a well
in the center of each roll; fill with one
tablespoon marmalade. Sprinkle rolls
with almonds. Bake at 400 degrees for
15 to 20 minutes, until golden. Cool
in pan 10 minutes. Mix almond extract
into reserved icing. Spread rolls
carefully with icing. Serve warm.
Makes 8 servings.

Jewel Sharpe
Raleigh, NC

These sweet rolls are our
favorite breakfast when we
go camping. Just a few extra
ingredients turn store-bought
rolls into homemade goodies!

Savory Breakfast Pancakes

2 c. biscuit baking mix
1 c. milk
2 eggs, beaten
1/2 c. shredded mozzarella cheese
1/2 c. pepperoni, chopped
1/2 c. tomato, chopped
1/4 c. green pepper, chopped
2 t. Italian seasoning
Garnish: pizza sauce, grated
   Parmesan cheese

Stir together baking mix, milk
and eggs until well blended; add
remaining ingredients except
garnish. Heat a lightly greased
griddle over medium-high heat.
Ladle batter by 1/4 cupfuls onto the
griddle; cook until golden on both
sides. Garnish with warmed pizza
sauce and Parmesan cheese. Makes
15 pancakes.

9

Jessica Parker
Mulvane, KS

Give the kids the unexpected
for breakfast...these will
disappear fast!

Nutty Brown Sugar Muffins

2 eggs, beaten
1/2 c. butter, melted and cooled
  slightly
1 c. brown sugar, packed
1/2 c. all-purpose flour
1 c. chopped pecans

Stir together eggs and butter. Add remaining ingredients; stir just until blended. Spray foil muffin cup liners with non-stick vegetable spray. Place liners in a muffin tin; fill 2/3 full. Bake at 350 degrees for 25 minutes. Remove muffins from pan immediately; cool. Makes 10.

Pearl Weaver
East Prairie, MO

With a flavor that's so much like pecan pie, these muffins are sure to become a new favorite.

Sunrise Pizza

8-oz. tube refrigerated
  crescent rolls
1 c. cooked ham, diced
1 c. frozen diced potatoes with
  onions and peppers
1 c. shredded sharp Cheddar
  cheese
4 eggs
3 T. milk
1/2 t. salt
1/4 t. pepper

Separate rolls into 4 rectangles.
Place on an ungreased baking sheet
or 12" round pizza pan. Build up
edges slightly to form a crust. Firmly
press perforations to seal. Sprinkle
ham evenly over crust. Top with
frozen vegetables and cheese. Beat
eggs; stir in milk, salt and pepper.
Pour egg mixture over cheese in
crust. Bake at 375 degrees for 15
minutes, or until center is set. Cut
into wedges to serve. Serves 6.

II

**Mary Lou Thomas
Portland, ME**
A quick recipe just right
for busy mornings. We wrap
up individual slices and pop
them in the microwave before
heading out the door!

Apple-Stuffed French Toast

3 apples, peeled, cored and cut
   into chunks
1/4 c. brown sugar, packed
cinnamon to taste
2 eggs, beaten
1/2 c. milk
1 t. vanilla extract
8 slices wheat bread
Garnish: maple syrup

In a microwave-safe bowl, combine
apples, brown sugar and cinnamon.
Cover and microwave on high for
5 minutes, until apples are soft. In a
separate bowl, stir together eggs, milk
and vanilla. Spray a griddle or large
frying pan with non-stick vegetable
spray and heat over medium heat.
Quickly dip the bread on both sides
in the egg mixture and place on the
griddle. Cook until golden on both
sides. Place one slice of toast on a
plate; put a scoop of the apple mixture
in the middle. Top with another slice
of toast. Drizzle with maple syrup.
Makes 4 servings.

Wendy Paffenroth
Pine Island, NY

Amazing aroma and divine
flavor...that's what
breakfast is all about!

Kitchen Café Mocha

Carrie O'Shea
Marina Del Rey, CA

Oh, café mocha is such a treat! I make this every Saturday to tote with me on errands.

6 c. hot brewed coffee
3/4 c. half-and-half
6 T. chocolate syrup
2 T. plus 1 t. sugar
Garnish: whipped cream,
    chocolate syrup

In a large saucepan, combine all ingredients except garnish. Cook and stir over medium heat until sugar is dissolved and mixture is heated through. Pour into mugs and garnish as desired. Makes 6 servings.

Peachy Waffle Topping

16-oz. can sliced peaches in
   heavy syrup
1 T. lemon juice
1 T. cornstarch

Strain syrup from peaches into a
saucepan. Cut peaches into bite-size
pieces and set aside. In a bowl, mix
lemon juice with cornstarch. Stir
lemon mixture into syrup in saucepan.
Cook and stir over medium heat for
one minute, or until thickened. Stir
in peach slices. Makes about 2 cups.

Tori Willis
Champaign, IL

I recently tried this recipe
for the first time...after
one bite, I thought,
"I've got to share this
with all my friends!"

No-Cook Strawberry Freezer Jam

7 c. strawberries, hulled
1-3/4 oz. pkg. light powdered
   pectin
1-3/4 c. sugar, divided
1 c. light corn syrup
8 1/2-pint freezer-safe plastic
   containers and lids, sterilized

Thoroughly crush strawberries in a
large bowl; set aside. Combine pectin
with 1/4 cup sugar. Gradually add
pectin mixture to strawberries,
stirring vigorously. Let stand for
30 minutes, stirring occasionally.
Add corn syrup; mix well. Gradually
stir in remaining sugar until
dissolved. Spoon into containers
leaving 1/2-inch headspace; secure
lids. Let stand overnight at room
temperature before freezing. May be
frozen up to one year. Store in
refrigerator up to 4 weeks after
opening. Makes 8 containers.

15

**Dianne Gregory
Sheridan, AR**

It's so simple to preserve
the sunny taste of fresh
strawberries! Spread over hot
biscuits, toast or yogurt.

Buttermilk Oven Pancakes

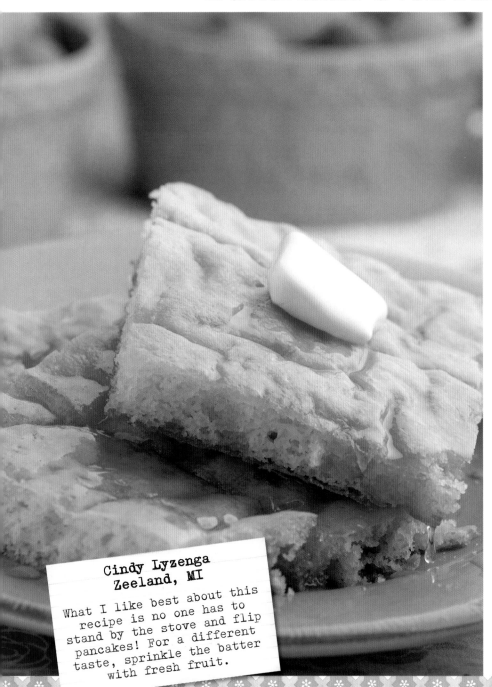

1-1/2 c. all-purpose flour
2 T. sugar
1 t. baking soda
1 t. baking powder
1/4 t. salt
1 egg, beaten
1-1/2 c. buttermilk
3 T. oil
cinnamon-sugar to taste
Garnish: butter, maple syrup

In a bowl, stir together flour, sugar, baking soda, baking powder and salt. In a separate bowl, combine egg, buttermilk and oil; add to dry ingredients. Stir just until mixed, but lightly lumpy. Spread batter evenly in a greased and floured 15"x10" jelly-roll pan. Sprinkle with cinnamon-sugar to taste. Bake at 350 degrees for 16 to 18 minutes, until top springs back when lightly touched and edges are lightly golden. Cut into squares and serve with butter and maple syrup. Makes 4 to 6 servings.

Cindy Lyzenga
Zeeland, MI

What I like best about this recipe is no one has to stand by the stove and flip pancakes! For a different taste, sprinkle the batter with fresh fruit.

Breakfast Bruschetta

1 c. red or green grapes, sliced
1 c. strawberries, hulled and
   sliced
1/4 t. cinnamon
1/8 t. nutmeg
1 c. cottage cheese or ricotta
1 T. chopped walnuts
1 baguette, cut in half lengthwise
   and sliced into 1-inch
   diagonals
2 to 3 T. olive oil

17

Place fruit in a small bowl; sprinkle with cinnamon and nutmeg. In another bowl, mix cheese and nuts. Brush bread lightly with olive oil and place on an ungreased baking sheet. Bake at 450 degrees until the bread turns golden, about 3 minutes. Remove from oven and spread cheese mixture on each piece of bread. Top with fruit mixture. Serves 4.

Jill Ball
Highland, UT

My family loves bruschetta, so I thought, why not have it for breakfast?

Slow-Cooker Hashbrown Casserole

32-oz. pkg. frozen shredded
   hashbrowns
1 lb. ground pork sausage,
   browned and drained
1 onion, diced
1 green pepper, diced
1-1/2 c. shredded Cheddar cheese
1 doz. eggs, beaten
1 c. milk
1 t. salt
1 t. pepper

Place 1/3 each of hashbrowns, sausage,
onion, green pepper and cheese in a
lightly greased slow cooker. Repeat
layering 2 more times, ending with
cheese. Beat eggs, milk, salt and pepper
together in a large bowl; pour over top.
Cover and cook on low setting for
10 hours. Serves 8.

Jessica Robertson
Fishers, IN

Sometimes I'll substitute
bacon or ham in place of the
sausage. This hearty recipe
works best in a large,
oval slow-cooker.

Ham & Feta Cheese Omelet

2 eggs, beaten
1/4 c. crumbled feta cheese
1/4 c. cucumber, diced
2 T. green onion, chopped
1/4 c. cooked ham, cubed
salt and pepper to taste
Garnish: salsa

Combine all ingredients except
salsa in a bowl; mix well. Pour into
a lightly greased sauté pan or small
skillet. Without stirring, cook over
low heat until set. Fold over; transfer
to serving plate. Serve with salsa.
Makes one serving.

19

Holly Jackson
Saint George, UT

All I can say
is, "Mmm!"

Good Morning Blueberry Shake

2-1/2 c. blueberries
1-1/4 c. apple juice
1 c. frozen vanilla yogurt
1/4 c. milk
3/4 t. cinnamon
Garnish: additional blueberries

Combine all ingredients except garnish in a blender and process until smooth. Garnish with additional blueberries. Serve immediately. Makes 4 servings.

Jo Ann

I enjoy a yummy breakfast shake...this drink blends up fast and is so pretty!

Easiest Cinnamon-Raisin Rolls

2 c. biscuit baking mix
1/2 c. raisins
1/2 c. sour cream
4 T. milk, divided
2 T. butter, softened
1/2 c. brown sugar, packed
1/4 c. nuts, finely chopped
1/2 t. cinnamon
1 c. powdered sugar

In a bowl, stir baking mix, raisins, sour cream and 3 tablespoons milk, just until combined. Gently smooth dough into a ball on a floured tea towel. Knead 10 times. Roll dough into a 12-inch by 10-inch rectangle. Spread rectangle with softened butter. Mix brown sugar, nuts and cinnamon; sprinkle over dough. Starting on the long end, roll up dough tightly; pinch edge to seal. Cut roll into 12 slices. Place slices, cut-side down, in greased muffin cups. Bake at 400 degrees for 15 minutes, or until golden. Stir together remaining milk and powdered sugar; drizzle over warm rolls. Makes one dozen.

21

Nola Coons
Gooseberry Patch

Brew a pot of coffee and share these wonderful rolls with your neighborhood pals.

Butterscotch Coffee Cake

18-1/2 oz. pkg. yellow cake mix
3.4-oz. pkg. instant vanilla
    pudding mix
3.4-oz. pkg. instant butterscotch
    pudding mix
4 eggs, beaten
1/2 c. oil
1 c. water
3/4 c. brown sugar, packed
3/4 c. chopped walnuts
1 t. cinnamon

With an electric mixer on medium speed, combine dry cake mix, dry pudding mixes, eggs, oil and water. Pour into a greased 13"x9" baking pan. Combine remaining ingredients and sprinkle over cake. Bake at 350 degrees for 40 minutes, or until toothpick tests clean. Let cool and cut into squares. Makes 12 servings.

Luann Hartzler
Creston, OH
A neighbor brought this coffee cake as a house-warming gift twenty years ago and it's been a favorite ever since. Moist and very flavorful!

Scott's Wonderful Waffles

1 c. milk
1/2 c. oil
3 eggs, beaten
1-1/2 c. cherry pie filling
18-1/2 oz. pkg. yellow cake mix
Garnish: butter, maple syrup

In a bowl, mix all ingredients except garnish. Refrigerate until waffle iron is ready. Ladle batter by 1/2 cupfuls onto a lightly greased preheated waffle iron; bake according to manufacturer's directions. Garnish as desired. Makes 8 to 10 waffles.

23

Sheila Murray
Tehachapi, CA

My son came up with this recipe and made it for the whole family. It was a great hit!

Trail Mix Bagels

8-oz. pkg. cream cheese, softened
1 T. lemon juice
1 t. lemon zest, grated
1/2 c. raisins
1 carrot, peeled and grated
1/3 c. trail mix, coarsely chopped,
   or sunflower kernels
4 bagels, split

Place cream cheese in a bowl. Add remaining ingredients except bagels; stir until well blended and creamy. Spread between sliced bagels and wrap up for the trail. Makes 4 servings.

Becky Drees
Pittsfield, MA

Perfect for an on-the-go breakfast, lunch or hike... a tasty energy boost!

Sweet & Spicy Bacon

1/2 c. brown sugar, packed
2 T. chili powder
1 t. ground cumin
1 t. cumin seed
1 t. ground coriander
1/4 t. cayenne pepper
10 thick slices bacon

Line a 15"x10" jelly-roll pan with aluminum foil. Place a wire rack on pan and set aside. Combine all ingredients except bacon; sprinkle mixture onto a large piece of wax paper. Press bacon into mixture, turning to coat well. Arrange in a single layer on prepared pan; place pan on center rack of oven. Bake at 400 degrees for 12 minutes; turn bacon over. Bake for an additional 10 minutes, until deep golden. Drain on paper towels; serve warm. Serves 4 to 5.

Zoe Bennett
Columbia, SC

Try this easy-to-fix bacon at your next brunch...guests will love it!

Cream Cheesy Strudel

2 8-oz. tubes refrigerated crescent
   rolls, divided
2 8-oz. pkgs. cream cheese,
   softened
1 egg, beaten
1/2 c. plus 2 T. sugar, divided
1 t. vanilla extract
1/4 t. cinnamon

Arrange one tube crescent rolls in the
bottom of an ungreased 13"x9" baking
pan. Mix cream cheese, egg, 1/2 cup
sugar and vanilla; spread over crescent
rolls. Cover with remaining crescent
rolls; sprinkle with cinnamon and
remaining sugar. Bake at 375 degrees
for 11 to 13 minutes. Cut into squares
to serve. Makes 1-1/2 to 2 dozen.

Donna Simonson
Sullivan, OH

Dress up this strudel for
the holidays! Just sprinkle
with colored sugar...red and
green for Christmas, yellow
and pink for Easter.

Make-Ahead Cheese & Egg Casserole

3 c. seasoned croutons
15 eggs, beaten
2 c. milk
1 t. seasoned salt
1 t. pepper
3/4 t. onion powder
2 T. fresh chives, chopped
1-1/2 c. shredded Cheddar
   cheese

Place croutons in a 13"x9" baking pan coated with non-stick vegetable spray. Whisk together eggs, milk and seasonings; stir in cheese. Pour over croutons. Cover and chill 8 hours, stirring once. Uncover and stir. Bake at 350 degrees for 30 minutes, or until set. Serves 8 to 10.

Irene Robinson
Cincinnati, OH

This overnight casserole is great for weekend breakfasts or a special brunch.

Balsamic Chicken & Pears

2 t. oil, divided
4 boneless, skinless chicken breasts
2 Bosc pears, cored and cut into
   8 wedges
1 c. chicken broth
3 T. balsamic vinegar
2 t. cornstarch
1-1/2 t. sugar
1/4 c. dried cherries or raisins

Heat one teaspoon oil in a large
non-stick skillet over medium-high
heat; add chicken. Cook until golden
and cooked through, about 4 to
5 minutes per side. Transfer to a plate;
keep warm. Heat remaining oil in same
skillet; add pears and cook until tender
and golden. In a small bowl, combine
remaining ingredients except cherries
or raisins. Stir broth mixture into
skillet with pears; add cherries or
raisins. Bring to a boil over medium
heat. Cook for one minute, stirring
constantly. Return chicken to pan;
heat through. Serve pear sauce over
chicken. Serves 4.

Shirl Parsons
Cape Carteret, NC

The flavors in this dish
blend together so well...
very, very tasty!

Italian Sausage Skillet

1-1/4 lb. pkg. Italian pork
   sausage links
3 zucchini, cubed
1/2 c. onion, chopped
14-1/2 oz. can stewed tomatoes
cooked pasta

In a skillet over medium heat, cook
sausage until no longer pink; drain.
Cut sausage into 1/4-inch slices;
return to skillet and cook until
browned. Add zucchini and onion;
cook and stir for 2 minutes. Stir
in tomatoes with juice. Reduce
heat; cover and simmer for 10 to
15 minutes, until zucchini is
tender. Serve over cooked pasta.
Serves 4 to 6.

29

Mary Gage
Wakewood, CA
Such a versatile dish...use
a combination of yellow
squash and zucchini
or serve over rice.

Asian Chicken Wraps

2 boneless, skinless chicken
  breasts, cooked and shredded
2/3 c. General Tso's sauce
1/4 c. teriyaki sauce
4 10-inch flour tortillas
10-oz. pkg. romaine and cabbage
  salad mix
1/2 c. carrot, peeled and shredded
1/4 c. sliced almonds
2 T. chow mein noodles

Combine chicken and sauces in a
skillet. Cook over medium heat until
heated through; remove from heat.
Divide ingredients evenly on each
tortilla, beginning with salad mix,
carrot, chicken mixture, almonds and
ending with chow mein noodles. Roll
up burrito style. Makes 4 servings.

Lisa Stanish
Houston, TX

These wraps are very easy
to prepare after a long day
at work. They're so much
tastier than fast food!

Jambalaya in a Jiff

2 T. butter
7-oz. pkg. chicken-flavored rice
  vermicelli mix
2-3/4 c. water
1/4 t. pepper
1/4 t. hot pepper sauce
1 T. dried, minced onion
1/4 c. celery, diced
1/4 c. green pepper, diced
2 c. cooked ham, diced
1 lb. cooked medium shrimp

Melt butter in a large saucepan over medium heat. Add rice vermicelli mix and sauté just until golden. Stir in remaining ingredients; reduce heat, cover and simmer for 15 minutes. Serves 4 to 6.

31

Patricia Perkins
Shenandoah, IA

Add a little more hot pepper sauce if you like it spicy!

Key West Burgers

Kimberly Ascroft
Merritt Island, FL

For a real Key West experience, enjoy these flavorful burgers with a frozen tropical drink!

1 lb. ground beef
3 T. Key lime juice
1/4 c. fresh cilantro, chopped
salt and pepper to taste
hamburger buns, split and toasted
Garnish: lettuce

In a bowl, combine ground beef, lime juice, cilantro, salt and pepper. Form beef mixture into 4 patties. Spray a large skillet with non-stick vegetable spray. Cook patties over medium heat for 6 minutes. Flip patties, cover skillet and cook for another 6 minutes. Place lettuce on bottom halves of buns and top with patties. Add Creamy Burger Spread onto bun tops and close sandwiches. Serves 4.

Creamy Burger Spread:

8-oz. pkg. cream cheese, softened
8-oz. container sour cream
3 green onion tops, chopped

Combine all ingredients until completely blended. Cover and refrigerate at least 15 minutes.

Unstuffed Green Pepper Soup

2 lbs. ground beef
2 10-3/4 oz. cans tomato soup
28-oz. can petite diced tomatoes
4-oz. can mushroom pieces,
    drained
2 c. green peppers, diced
1 c. onion, diced
1/4 c. brown sugar, packed
3 to 4 c. beef broth
2 c. cooked rice

In a stockpot over medium heat, brown ground beef; drain. Stir in soup, vegetables and brown sugar. Add desired amount of beef broth. Simmer, covered, until peppers and onion are tender, about 30 minutes. Stir in rice about 5 minutes before serving. Makes 8 servings.

33

Peggy Cantrell
Okmulgee, OK

This soup is right up there on my list of comfort foods! All the flavors of a stuffed green pepper without the work.

Company's Coming Pork Chops

4 to 6 boneless pork chops
salt and pepper to taste
1/4 c. olive oil
1 c. white wine or chicken broth
4 to 5 green onions, chopped
1 t. dried thyme
1 c. milk
1 t. cornstarch

Season pork chops with salt and pepper. Heat oil in a skillet over medium-high heat. Brown pork chops on both sides, turning once; drain. Add wine or broth to the pan and use a wooden spoon to scrape up the drippings. Stir in onions and thyme. Reduce heat to medium-low and simmer until liquid is reduced, about 5 minutes. Whisk milk and cornstarch together and pour over chops. Simmer, stirring occasionally for 15 minutes, or until sauce is thickened. Remove chops from pan; serve with sauce. Serves 4 to 6.

Nancy Cowling
DeQueen, AR

I love to make this recipe on a busy weeknight. Tastes and looks special, but it's fast and easy!

Easy Skillet Lasagna

1-1/2 T. olive oil
1/2 green pepper, finely chopped
1 onion, finely chopped
1 clove garlic, minced
16-oz. jar spaghetti sauce
1 lb. ground beef, browned and
    drained
6 lasagna noodles, cooked and
    cut in half
12-oz. container small-curd
    cottage cheese
4 slices mozzarella cheese
1/2 c. Parmesan cheese

35

Heat oil in a skillet over medium heat. Sauté green pepper, onion and garlic until tender; drain. Transfer to a bowl; stir in spaghetti sauce and browned beef. In skillet, layer 1/3 of sauce mixture, half the lasagna noodles, half the cottage cheese, 2 slices of mozzarella and half the Parmesan. Repeat layers. Top with remaining sauce, making sure to cover all noodles. Cover and simmer over medium-low heat for 10 to 15 minutes. Remove from heat and let stand for 10 minutes before uncovering and serving. Serves 4.

Terri McClure
Hilliard, OH

My husband often asks me to make this recipe. And sometimes, he even helps prepare it! Tastes great with ground turkey too.

Salmon Cornbread Cakes

2 T. mayonnaise
2 eggs, beaten
1 t. dried parsley
3 green onions, thinly sliced
1 t. seafood seasoning
1 to 2 t. Worcestershire sauce
14-3/4 oz. can salmon, drained
    and bones removed
2 c. cornbread, crumbled
1 T. canola oil

Combine mayonnaise, eggs, parsley, green onions, seafood seasoning and Worcestershire sauce. Mix well. Mix in salmon and cornbread. Shape into 6 to 8 patties. Heat oil in a skillet over medium heat. Cook patties for 3 to 4 minutes on each side, until golden. Serves 6.

Lorrie Smith
Drummonds, TN

A different take on traditional salmon croquettes. I absolutely love these!

Hug in a Mug Soup

1 lb. ground turkey
1 T. butter
1 onion, chopped
3 cloves garlic, minced
1 green pepper, chopped
1.35-oz. pkg. onion soup mix
16-oz. can navy beans, drained
   and rinsed
16-oz. can kidney beans, drained
   and rinsed
28-oz. can crushed tomatoes
28-oz. can diced tomatoes,
   drained
1 T. dried parsley
1 T. dried basil
8 c. water
salt and pepper to taste
1 c. small pasta shells, uncooked

In a stockpot over medium heat,
brown turkey; drain and set aside. In
the same pot, melt butter over
medium heat; sauté onion, garlic and
green pepper until tender. Add
remaining ingredients except pasta
and bring to a boil. Stir in pasta.
Simmer, uncovered, over medium
heat for 10 minutes, or until pasta is
tender. Serves 8.

37

Michelle Marberry
Valley, AL

A quick-to-fix family
favorite! Serve in big soup
mugs with a hearty bread for
a very comforting supper.

Saucy Slow-Cooker Pulled Pork

1 T. barbecue spice rub
4-lb. boneless pork shoulder
1-1/2 yellow onions, sliced
2 16-oz. cans whole-berry
   cranberry sauce
18-oz. bottle barbecue sauce
6 to 8 sandwich rolls, split

Pat spice rub onto pork shoulder. Wrap pork in plastic wrap and refrigerate overnight. Add onions to a slow cooker and place unwrapped pork on top. In a bowl, combine cranberry sauce and barbecue sauce. Pour sauce mixture over pork. Cover and cook on low setting for 8 to 10 hours. Remove pork to a bowl and shred with 2 forks. Strain about 1-1/2 cups sauce from the slow cooker and stir into shredded pork. Serve on sandwich rolls. Serves 6 to 8.

Karen Christiansen
Glenview, IL
I overheard part of this recipe while standing in the checkout line at the grocery store! I only knew some ingredients, so I came up with my own version.

Spicy Salsa Twists

1 lb. ground beef, browned and
  drained
8-oz. pkg. rotini pasta, cooked
10-3/4 oz. can tomato soup
1 c. salsa
1/2 c. milk
1 c. shredded Cheddar cheese,
  divided
Optional: sour cream, tortilla
  chips

Combine browned beef, rotini,
soup, salsa, milk and 1/2 cup cheese
in a large skillet. Cook over medium
heat until heated through and cheese
is melted; sprinkle with remaining
cheese. Serve with sour cream and
tortilla chips, if desired. Serves 5.

39

Heather Jacobson
Galesville, WI
A wonderful dish that's
big on flavor and cooks up
in a snap!

Skillet Dinner

1 lb. ground beef
1 onion, chopped
14-1/2 oz. can beef broth
2/3 c. water
1 c. long-cooking rice, uncooked
1/2 t. dry mustard
1 green pepper, chopped
1 tomato, chopped
1 c. shredded Pepper Jack cheese

Brown ground beef and onion in a large skillet over medium heat; drain. Stir in broth, water, rice and dry mustard; bring to a boil. Reduce heat; simmer, uncovered, until liquid is absorbed, about 25 minutes. Stir in green pepper and tomato; sprinkle cheese over top. Cover and remove from heat. Let stand for 2 to 3 minutes, until cheese melts. Serves 4 to 6.

Denise Oravecz
Pittsburgh, PA

Hearty and filling...a real family-pleaser!

Mandy's Hand-Battered Chicken

1-1/2 lbs. boneless, skinless
   chicken breast tenders
3 c. self-rising flour
2 T. salt
1 T. pepper
2 t. garlic powder
dried parsley to taste
2 c. cold milk
oil for deep frying
Optional: additional dried
   parsley

Pat chicken dry. Combine flour and seasonings in a large bowl. Add milk to a separate bowl. Working with several pieces at a time, dip chicken into milk and then dredge in flour mixture. Set aside. Cover the bottom of a 12" skillet with oil; heat over medium heat until hot, about 3 to 4 minutes. Place chicken tenders in skillet and fry until crisp on one side; turn over. Continue frying until golden and crisp on all sides and juices run clear when chicken is pierced with a fork. Be careful not to overcook. Remove from skillet and drain on a paper-towel lined plate. Garnish with additional parsley, if desired. Serves 4.

41

Amanda Johnson
Marysville, OH

This is a recipe I whipped up one day when our pantry was running low with supplies. It's simple but makes the best chicken tenders. Dip in your favorite sauce!

Lemony "Baked" Chicken

3 to 4-lb. roasting chicken
2 T. olive oil
1 lemon
2 cloves garlic, minced
1 t. dried parsley
salt and pepper to taste

Pat chicken dry with a paper towel; rub with oil. Put whole lemon inside chicken; place in a slow cooker. Sprinkle with seasonings. Cover and cook on high setting for one hour. Turn to low setting and cook an additional 6 to 7 hours. Makes 4 servings.

Sharon Lundberg
Longwood, FL

Stir a little lemon zest and chopped parsley into steamed rice for a perfect side dish. Choose a large, oval slow cooker for this recipe.

Sunday Meatball Skillet

3/4 lb. ground beef
1 c. onion, grated
1/2 c. Italian-flavored dry bread
  crumbs
1 egg, beaten
1/4 c. catsup
1/4 t. pepper
2 c. beef broth
1/4 c. all-purpose flour
1/2 c. sour cream
8-oz. pkg. medium egg noodles,
  cooked
Garnish: chopped fresh parsley

43

In a bowl, combine beef, onion, bread crumbs, egg, catsup and pepper. Shape into one-inch meatballs. Spray a skillet with non-stick vegetable spray. Cook meatballs over medium heat, turning occasionally, until browned, about 10 minutes. Remove meatballs and let drain on paper towels. In a bowl, whisk together broth and flour; add to skillet. Cook and stir until mixture thickens, about 5 minutes. Stir in sour cream. Add meatballs and noodles; toss to coat. Cook and stir until heated through, about 5 minutes. Garnish with parsley. Serves 4.

Doris Stegner
Gooseberry Patch

Oh-so delicious alongside roasted green beans and a bowl of homemade applesauce!

Penne & Spring Vegetables

16-oz. pkg. penne pasta, uncooked
1 lb. asparagus, cut into 1/2-inch
  pieces
1/2 lb. sugar snap peas
3 T. olive oil
1/2 c. grated Parmesan cheese
salt and pepper to taste

Cook pasta according to package
directions. Add asparagus during the
last 4 minutes of cook time; add peas
during the last 2 minutes of cook time.
Remove pot from heat; drain pasta
mixture and return to pot. Toss with
remaining ingredients; serve warm.
Serves 4 to 6.

Denise Piccirilli
Huber Heights, OH

A delicious meatless main
or a tasty side for
grilled chicken.

Chicken & Peppers Stir-Fry

1/2 c. soy sauce
2 T. sesame oil
1 T. catsup
4 cloves garlic, minced
4 boneless, skinless chicken
   breasts, cut into 1-inch pieces
1/2 red pepper, chopped
1/2 yellow pepper, chopped
cooked rice

In a bowl, whisk together soy sauce, oil, catsup and garlic. Heat mixture in a skillet over medium-high heat. Add chicken; cook and stir for 3 minutes. Add peppers; cook and stir 5 minutes, or until chicken is cooked through. Serve over hot rice. Serves 4.

45

Regina Wickline
Pebble Beach, CA

I was inspired to create this colorful and yummy recipe after falling in love with a similar dish at my favorite downtown restaurant.

Apple-Stuffed Turkey Breast

1-1/2 c. long grain & wild rice,
  uncooked
2 apples, peeled, cored and
  chopped
1 onion, finely chopped
1/2 c. sweetened dried cranberries
3 c. water
4 to 5-lb. boneless, skinless turkey
  breast

Combine rice, apples, onion and
cranberries in a slow cooker; pour
water over top. Mix well. Place turkey
on top of rice mixture. Cover and
cook on low setting for 8 to 9 hours.
Serves 10.

Dale Duncan
Waterloo, IA
The combination of wild rice,
apples and cranberries
really gives this turkey
an amazing flavor.

Hearty Chicken-Bacon Melts

4 boneless, skinless chicken
  breasts
1 onion, sliced
2 t. margarine
2 t. olive oil
4 slices bread, toasted
4 t. steak sauce
8 slices bacon, crisply cooked
1 c. shredded Cheddar cheese

Place chicken between pieces of wax paper and flatten to about 1/4-inch thickness. In a large skillet, cook onion in margarine and oil until softened. Remove onion from skillet. Add chicken to skillet; cook for about 7 to 9 minutes on each side, until cooked through. Place toasted bread slices on a large baking sheet; spread each slice with one teaspoon steak sauce. Top each with a chicken breast, 2 slices bacon, 1/4 of onion slices and 1/4 cup cheese. Broil 4 to 6 inches from heat for one to 2 minutes, until cheese is melted. Serves 4.

47

Vickie

A warm, melty open-face sandwich you need to eat with a fork!

Creamy Chicken Bake

2 c. elbow macaroni, uncooked
1 c. mayonnaise
10-3/4 oz. can cream of chicken
    soup
1-1/2 c. cooked chicken, chopped
2 c. grated Parmesan cheese
1/4 c. chopped pimentos
1/4 c. onion, chopped
1/2 c. potato chips, crushed

Cook macaroni according to package
instructions; drain. Meanwhile, in a
bowl, combine mayonnaise, soup
and chicken. Stir in macaroni and
remaining ingredients except potato
chips. Transfer to a lightly greased
13"x9" baking pan; sprinkle with
potato chips. Bake, uncovered, at
375 degrees for 30 minutes, or
until bubbly. Serves 4 to 6.

April Jacobs
Loveland, CO

When my picky eaters
are away, I'll stir
in my favorite
ingredients...mushrooms
and chopped green pepper!

Chili & Biscuits

Lisa Hains
Ontario, Canada

This dish was created by combining two family favorites into one easy dinner. If you're in a hurry, bake the biscuits separately while the chili is simmering.

1 lb. ground beef
1 onion, chopped
4 stalks celery, chopped
1-1/4 oz. pkg. chili seasoning mix
1/4 c. all-purpose flour
28-oz. can diced tomatoes
15-1/2 oz. can chili beans
Optional: 4-oz. can sliced
    mushrooms, drained
garlic powder and salt and
    pepper to taste

In a large skillet, brown together beef, onion and celery. Drain; stir in chili seasoning and flour. Add remaining ingredients and simmer until thickened and bubbly. Transfer to a lightly greased 13"x9" baking pan. Drop Biscuit Dough by tablespoonfuls over the hot chili. Bake, uncovered, at 375 degrees for 10 to 15 minutes, until biscuits are golden. Serves 6 to 8.

Biscuit Dough:

1-1/2 c. all-purpose flour
1 c. yellow cornmeal
4 t. baking powder
1/2 t. salt
2 T. sugar
1/2 c. oil
1/2 to 3/4 c. milk

Combine dry ingredients and oil. Stir in enough milk to form a soft dough.

Poor Man's Steak & Vegetables

6 ground beef patties
4 potatoes, peeled and cubed
3 carrots, peeled and diced
1 onion, quartered or sliced
salt and pepper to taste

Place patties in a greased 13"x9" baking pan. Evenly arrange vegetables over patties. Sprinkle with salt and pepper to taste. Bake, covered, at 400 degrees for 45 to 50 minutes, or until beef is no longer pink and potatoes are tender. Serves 6.

Cynthia Armstrong
Big Stone Gap, VA

This recipe has been handed down for several generations. My mother used to serve this dish when money was tight. It has become a family favorite!

Zippy Broiled Catfish

6 catfish fillets
1/4 c. lemon juice
1 t. salt
1/8 t. pepper
1 c. all-purpose flour
1-1/3 c. Italian salad dressing

Brush fillets with lemon juice;
sprinkle with salt and pepper.
Dredge fillets in flour. Arrange on
a well-greased broiler pan; brush
with salad dressing. Broil about
4 inches from heat source for 4 to
6 minutes, basting occasionally
with salad dressing. Turn carefully;
brush with additional salad dressing.
Broil for an additional 4 to
6 minutes, until fish flakes easily.
Serves 6.

51

Mardell Ross
Genoa, IL

Pop this in the oven and
by the time you toss the
salad and set the table,
dinner is served!

Parmesan Baked Chicken

Gina Powell
Gadsden, AL

I tried this hand-me-down recipe when I was looking for something different to make with chicken. The bottom of the chicken will be more browned than the top.

1/2 c. butter, melted
1 clove garlic, minced
1 c. Italian-flavored dry bread
  crumbs
1/3 c. grated Parmesan cheese
2 T. fresh parsley
1/4 t. salt
1/4 t. garlic powder
pepper to taste
Optional: 1/2 t. Italian seasoning
4 to 6 boneless, skinless chicken
  breasts

In a bowl, combine butter and garlic. In another bowl, combine bread crumbs, Parmesan cheese and seasonings. Dip chicken in butter mixture to coat; dredge in bread crumb mixture. Place chicken into an ungreased 13"x9" baking pan. Drizzle remaining butter mixture over chicken. Bake, uncovered, at 400 degrees for 20 to 25 minutes, until juices run clear when pierced. Makes 4 to 6 servings.

Cheesy Ham & Vegetable Bake

1-1/2 c. rotini pasta, uncooked
16-oz. pkg. frozen broccoli,
  carrots and cauliflower blend
1/2 c. sour cream
1/2 c. milk
1-1/2 c. shredded Cheddar
  cheese, divided
1-1/2 c. cooked ham, chopped
1/4 c. onion, chopped
1 clove garlic, minced
1/2 c. croutons, crushed

Cook pasta according to package directions; add frozen vegetables to cooking water just to thaw. Drain; place mixture in a 2-quart casserole dish that has been sprayed with non-stick vegetable spray. Mix sour cream, milk, one cup cheese, ham, onion and garlic; stir into pasta mixture in dish. Bake, uncovered, at 350 degrees for 30 minutes. Sprinkle with croutons and remaining cheese during last 5 minutes of baking. Serves 6.

53

Jackie Flood
Geneseo, NY

A good way to use up leftover ham after Easter or other holiday occasions! If you prefer a lighter version, low-fat or fat-free products work fine in this recipe.

Foil-Wrapped Baked Salmon

4 salmon fillets
1 onion, sliced
1/4 c. butter, diced
1 lemon, thinly sliced
1/4 c. brown sugar, packed

Place each fillet on a piece of aluminum foil that has been sprayed with non-stick vegetable spray. Top fillets evenly with onion slices, diced butter, lemon slices and brown sugar. Fold over aluminum foil tightly to make packets; make several holes in top of packets with a fork to allow steam to escape. Arrange packets on an ungreased baking sheet. Bake at 375 degrees for 15 to 20 minutes. Serves 4.

Katherine Murnane
Plattsburgh, NY

These packets can also be cooked on a hot grill. Delightful with a salad of fresh garden greens.

Beef & Potato Roll

2 lbs. ground beef
2 t. salt
1/8 t. pepper
1 T. Worcestershire sauce
1 onion, chopped
1 egg, slightly beaten
3 slices bacon, crisply cooked
   and crumbled
3 c. mashed potatoes

In a bowl, combine all ingredients except potatoes, mixing well. Place mixture onto wax paper and shape into a rectangle approximately 1/4" thick. Mound potatoes down the center of the rectangle. Use the edges of the wax paper to wrap beef around the potatoes. Press beef edges together to seal tightly. Place roll, seam-side down, into an ungreased 11"x7" baking pan; remove wax paper. Bake, uncovered, at 350 degrees for 35 to 40 minutes, or until beef is done. Slice into portions. Serves 6 to 8.

55

Andrea Ford
Montfort, WI
This recipe was handed down from my grandma. My mom used to double the recipe for the farmhands during haying season.

Easy Sweet-and-Sour Chicken

8-oz. bottle Russian salad dressing
1-1/2 oz. pkg. onion soup mix
1/3 c. apricot jam
2-1/2 to 3 lbs. boneless, skinless
   chicken breasts
Optional: chopped green onions

Whisk first 3 ingredients in a mixing
bowl; set aside. Arrange chicken in an
ungreased 13"x9" baking pan; pour
dressing mixture on top. Bake,
covered, at 350 degrees for 50 minutes
to one hour, until juices run clear
when chicken is pierced with a fork. If
desired, cut chicken into strips before
serving and garnish with green onions.
Makes 4 to 6 servings.

Sandra Nakagawa
Honolulu, HI
Served on a bed of rice or
crunchy chow mein noodles,
this is a meal the whole
family will love.

Dill Rice & Chicken

1-1/2 c. sour cream
2 10-3/4 oz. cans cream of
    chicken soup
2-1/2 c. cooked chicken, diced
1-1/2 c. quick-cooking rice,
    uncooked
1 c. shredded Cheddar cheese
1 t. poppy seed
1-1/4 t. dill weed
1/4 t. onion salt
1/4 t. garlic salt

Combine all ingredients and transfer
to an ungreased 13"x9" baking pan.
Bake, uncovered, at 350 degrees
for 20 minutes. Sprinkle with Crumb
Topping and bake 10 minutes longer.
Makes 10 to 12 servings.

Crumb Topping:

Optional: 1/2 c. sliced almonds,
    toasted
1-1/2 c. buttery rectangular
    crackers, crushed
1/2 c. butter, melted

Combine all ingredients.

57

**Elisabeth Miller
Rocky Mount, VA**
This creamy casserole makes
a great dish to carry on a
picnic or even to a potluck.

Apricot-Glazed Ham Steaks

1/4 c. apricot preserves
1 T. mustard
1 t. lemon juice
1/8 t. cinnamon
4 ham steaks

In a small saucepan, combine all ingredients except ham. Cook and stir over low heat for 2 to 3 minutes. Place ham in a lightly greased 13"x9" baking dish. Pour sauce over ham. Bake, uncovered, at 350 degrees for 15 minutes, or until heated through. Serve ham topped with sauce from the pan. Makes 4 servings.

Kelly Alderson
Erie, PA

When it's grilling season, heat the ham over hot coals and serve with grilled apricot halves...oh-so good!

Down-Home Taco Casserole

1 lb. ground beef, browned and
   drained
10-3/4 oz. can tomato soup
1 c. salsa
1/2 c. milk
8-1/2 oz. can peas & carrots,
   drained
7 6-inch corn tortillas, cut into
   1-inch squares
1-1/2 t. chili powder
1 c. shredded Cheddar cheese,
   divided

59

Combine all ingredients except
1/2 cup cheese; spread in a 2-quart
casserole dish sprayed with non-stick
vegetable spray. Cover and bake at
400 degrees for 30 minutes, or until
hot. Sprinkle with remaining cheese;
let stand until cheese melts. Makes
4 servings.

Kathy Goscha
Topeka, KS

A south-of-the border dish
with a country twist!

Baked Pork Medallions

1/2 c. grated Parmesan cheese
.6-oz. pkg. Italian salad dressing
 mix
1/4 c. red wine vinegar
2 T. olive oil
2 lbs. pork tenderloin, sliced into
 1-inch-thick medallions
cooked fettuccine pasta
Garnish: chopped fresh chives

In a bowl, combine Parmesan cheese
and salad dressing mix. In a separate
bowl, whisk vinegar and oil. Dip
medallions into vinegar mixture, then
into Parmesan mixture. Place in an
ungreased 13"x9" baking pan. Bake,
uncovered, at 375 degrees for 30 to
35 minutes, until cooked through.
Serve over pasta and garnish with
chives. Serves 6 to 8.

Claire Bertram
Lexington, KY

My mother-in-law makes these
fantastic medallions every
New Year's Day. One more
reason to celebrate!

Speedy Steak & Veggies

juice of 1 lime
salt and pepper to taste
1-1/2 lb. beef flank steak
1/2 bunch broccoli, cut into
    flowerets
2 c. baby carrots, sliced
2 ears corn, husked and cut into
    2-inch pieces
1 red onion, sliced into wedges
2 T. olive oil

61

Combine lime juice, salt and
pepper; brush over both sides of
beef. Place on a broiler pan and
broil, 5 minutes per side, turning
once. Set aside on a cutting board;
keep warm. Toss broccoli, carrots,
corn and onion with oil. Spoon onto
a lightly greased baking sheet in a
single layer. Bake at 475 degrees,
turning once, until tender, about
10 minutes. Slice steak into thin
strips on the diagonal and arrange on
a platter. Surround with vegetables.
Serves 4 to 6.

Jo Ann
A summertime favorite. We
find outstanding sweet corn
at our local farmers' market!

Little Meatloaves

1 egg, lightly beaten
1 c. pasta sauce, divided
1/2 c. dry bread crumbs
1/4 t. salt
1/4 c. fresh basil, coarsely chopped
  and divided
1 lb. ground beef
1 c. shredded mozzarella cheese

In a bowl, combine egg, 1/2 cup pasta
sauce, bread crumbs, salt and half the
basil. Add beef and 1/2 cup cheese;
mix well. Shape into 4, 5-1/2 by
2-inch ovals. Place in a lightly greased
13"x9" baking pan. Spoon remaining
sauce over top and sprinkle with
remaining cheese. Bake, uncovered, at
450 degrees for 15 minutes. Sprinkle
with remaining basil. Serves 4.

Tara Horton
Gooseberry Patch
Italian-style meatloaf for a
family of four in less than
half an hour? Oh, yes!

Jax's Cheeseburger Pizzas

1 lb. ground turkey
1/2 c. onion, diced
1/2 t. garlic salt
1/2 t. pepper
2 12-inch Italian pizza crusts
catsup and mustard to taste
16-oz. jar sliced bread & butter
   pickles, drained
8-oz. pkg. shredded Cheddar
   cheese

In a skillet over medium heat, brown turkey and onion; sprinkle with garlic salt and pepper. Drain and set aside. Place pizza crusts on ungreased baking sheets. Swirl catsup onto crusts, as you would do on a hamburger bun. Swirl mustard on top of the catsup (no need to smooth out or mix together). Divide turkey mixture evenly between the 2 crusts; arrange pickles on top of turkey. Sprinkle evenly with cheese. Bake at 425 degrees for 12 to 15 minutes, until cheese has melted. Cut into wedges to serve. Makes 2 pizzas, 8 servings each.

63

Jackie Daunce
Lockport, NY

This is a fast and easy supper I whip up for my husband and two boys. There are never any leftovers!

Mexicana Veggie Bake

1/2 c. green pepper, finely
   chopped
1/2 c. carrot, peeled and finely
   chopped
1/2 c. celery, finely chopped
1/2 c. onion, finely chopped
2 c. cooked rice
16-oz. can refried beans
15-oz. can black beans, drained
   and rinsed
1 c. salsa
12-oz. pkg. shredded Cheddar
   cheese, divided

Sauté vegetables in a lightly greased
skillet over medium heat for 5 minutes,
or until tender. Remove vegetables to a
large bowl; add remaining ingredients
except cheese. Layer half of mixture in
a lightly greased 13"x9" baking pan;
sprinkle with half the cheese. Repeat
layering, ending with cheese. Bake,
uncovered, at 350 degrees until heated
through, about 15 to 20 minutes.
Serves 6.

**Tawnia Hultink
Ontario, Canada**
Go meatless with layers
of tasty sautéed vegetables
and melted cheese.

Patsy's Stuffed Pork Chops

2 6-oz. pkgs. stuffing mix
8 boneless pork chops
2 T. oil
3 cloves garlic, sliced
salt and pepper to taste
2 c. applesauce
cinnamon to taste

Prepare stuffing mixes according to package instructions; set aside. Slicing horizontally into the sides, cut a pocket into the center of each pork chop. Evenly stuff chops with prepared stuffing. Drizzle oil and sprinkle garlic in a 13"x9" baking pan. Arrange chops in pan and season with salt and pepper. Top each chop with 1/4 cup applesauce and sprinkle with cinnamon. Bake, uncovered, at 425 degrees for 30 minutes, or until chops are no longer pink. Makes 8 servings.

65

Patricia Flaherty
Bergenfield, NJ

Prepare for raves and recipe requests when you serve these tasty chops!

Potluck Beef Sandwiches

1 lb. ground beef
1/4 onion, chopped
salt and pepper to taste
2/3 c. barbecue sauce
2 8-oz. tubes refrigerated
    crescent rolls
1/2 to 1 c. shredded Cheddar
    cheese
Garnish: additional barbecue
    sauce

In a skillet over medium heat, brown
beef and onion. Add a little salt and
pepper; drain. Mix in barbecue sauce.
Place crescent rolls on a baking sheet
and make a rectangle, pinching seams
together. Spoon beef mixture down
center of dough and sprinkle with
cheese. Fold the sides over and seal
dough down the center. Bake at
375 degrees for 20 minutes, or until
golden. Slice into portions and serve
with additional barbecue sauce.
Serves 4.

Carmen Chandler
Roseburg, OR

I tried this recipe when I
was first married, almost
thirty years ago. I didn't
know how to cook and this one
turned out well every time!

Honey Cornmeal Chicken

1/2 c. honey, divided
4 boneless, skinless chicken
  breasts
1/4 c. yellow cornmeal
1/2 t. orange zest

Spray an 11"x7" baking pan with
non-stick vegetable spray. Drizzle
about 2 tablespoons honey onto the
bottom of the pan; spread to lightly
cover. Arrange chicken in dish and
spread remaining honey over top.
Mix together cornmeal and orange
zest; sprinkle evenly over chicken.
Cover and bake at 350 degrees for
15 minutes. Remove pan from oven.
Uncover and spray tops of chicken
with non-stick vegetable spray.
Return to oven and bake, uncovered,
for an additional 30 minutes, or
until juices run clear when pierced.
Serves 4.

67

Bonnie Hudson
Clearfield, PA

A four-ingredient recipe
that tastes like a
five-star winner!

Corn Surprise

15-1/4 oz. can corn
8-oz. pkg. small pasta shells,
   uncooked
16-oz. can cream-style corn
8-oz. pkg. shredded
   Mexican-blend cheese

Combine undrained corn and
remaining ingredients in a bowl.
Transfer to a greased 13"x9" baking
pan. Bake, covered, at 350 degrees for
45 minutes, or until pasta is tender.
As it bakes, stir casserole several times;
uncover for the last 10 minutes of
cooking. Serves 6 to 8.

Eva Rae Walters
Paola, KS

A winter warm-up recipe
that's easy to double,
making it perfect for
potlucks.

Tangy Watermelon Salad

14 c. watermelon, cubed
1 red onion, halved and thinly
    sliced
1 c. green onions, chopped
3/4 c. orange juice
5 T. red wine vinegar
2 T. plus 1-1/2 t. honey
1 T. green pepper, finely
    chopped
1/2 t. salt
1/4 t. pepper
1/4 t. garlic powder
1/4 t. onion powder
1/4 t. dry mustard
3/4 c. oil

In a large bowl, combine watermelon and onion; set aside. In a small bowl, combine orange juice, vinegar, honey, green pepper and seasonings; slowly whisk in oil. Pour over watermelon mixture; toss gently. Cover and refrigerate for at least 2 hours. Serve with a slotted spoon. Makes about 10 servings.

69

Belva Conner
Hillsdale, IN

I won first prize for this recipe at our county fair. Everyone is surprised to see watermelon and onions together, but they always ask for the recipe!

Ripe Tomato Tart

9-inch pie crust
1-1/2 c. shredded mozzarella
    cheese, divided
4 roma tomatoes, cut into wedges
3/4 c. fresh basil, chopped
4 cloves garlic, minced
1/2 c. mayonnaise
1/2 c. grated Parmesan cheese
1/8 t. white pepper

Line an ungreased 9" tart pan with pie crust; press crust into fluted sides of pan and trim edges. Bake at 450 degrees for 5 to 7 minutes; remove from oven. Sprinkle with 1/2 cup mozzarella cheese; let cool on a wire rack. Combine remaining ingredients; mix well and fill crust. Reduce heat to 375 degrees; bake for about 20 minutes, or until bubbly on top. Makes 6 servings.

Darlene Lohrman
Chicago, IL

Fresh roma tomatoes are available year 'round so you can enjoy this summery-tasting pie anytime.

Raspberry Spinach Salad

6-oz. pkg. baby spinach
1 pt. raspberries
1 c. pecan pieces
1/4 c. red onion, finely chopped
2 kiwis, peeled and cubed
1/2 c. raspberry vinaigrette salad
   dressing

In a large bowl, toss together all
ingredients. Serve immediately.
Serves 4.

71

**Laina Lamb
Marion, OH**

I've never met anyone who
didn't love this salad.
Excellent for picnics...just
toss when you get there!

Pamela's Garlic Bread

8-oz. pkg. cream cheese, softened
4-oz. can chopped black olives,
   drained
4 green onions, chopped
2 to 3 cloves garlic, finely chopped
1/4 c. Italian seasoning
1/4 c. butter, softened
1 loaf French bread, halved
   lengthwise

In a bowl, combine all ingredients
except bread; mix until well blended.
Evenly spread mixture on bread halves.
Place on an ungreased baking sheet.
Bake at 350 degrees for 10 to
15 minutes. Let cool and slice.
Makes 12 servings.

Pamela Delacruz
Mount Vernon, WA

At our home church meetings,
people hover around the
kitchen waiting for this to
come out of the oven! You
can also use store-bought
garlic bread...just omit the
garlic and butter.

Fried Spaghetti

12-oz. pkg. thin spaghetti,
   uncooked
3 T. sesame oil
1/2 onion, chopped
1/4 c. frozen peas
1/4 c. bacon bits
2 T. soy sauce
2 T. teriyaki sauce

Cook spaghetti according to package directions; drain. Meanwhile, in a large saucepan, heat oil over medium heat. Sauté onion, frozen peas and bacon bits for 3 minutes, or until onion is soft. Stir in soy sauce, teriyaki sauce and spaghetti. Mix everything well. Cook for 5 minutes, stirring occasionally. Serves 4.

73

Tiffany Jones
Locust Grove, AR

My dad and I love Chinese food. I tried spaghetti noodles instead of rice...it turned out to be a favorite!

Sour Cream Cornbread

Dueley Lucas
Somerset, KY
This is the most-requested bread at all of our church dinners!

1-1/2 c. self-rising cornmeal
2 T. self-rising flour
1/4 c. sugar
2 eggs, beaten
1-1/2 c. sour cream
2/3 c. oil
1/2 c. buttermilk

Combine all ingredients in a large bowl and mix well. Pour into a greased 9"x9" baking pan. Bake at 350 degrees for 25 to 30 minutes, until golden. Makes 9 servings.

Spiced Baked Fruit

16-oz. can apricot halves,
   drained
16-oz. can pear halves, drained
29-oz. can peach halves, drained
8-oz. can pineapple slices,
   drained and 1/2 c. juice
   reserved
1/3 c. brown sugar, packed
1 T. butter
1/2 t. cinnamon
1/4 t. ground cloves

In a greased 13"x9" baking pan,
starting at the short end, arrange
rows of fruit in the following order:
half the apricots, half the pears and
half the peaches. Repeat rows.
Arrange pineapple over fruit. In a
saucepan over medium heat, combine
reserved pineapple juice and
remaining ingredients. Cook and
stir until sugar is dissolved and butter
is melted. Pour over fruit. Bake,
uncovered, at 350 degrees for 20 to
25 minutes, until heated through.
Serves 6 to 8.

75

Regina Ferrigno
Gooseberry Patch

Guests "ooh" and "ahh"
when they discover the
rows of fruit under the
pineapple...so pretty!

Spicy Carrot French Fries

2 lbs. carrots, peeled and cut into
  matchsticks
4 T. olive oil, divided
1 T. seasoned salt
2 t. ground cumin
1 t. chili powder
1 t. pepper
Garnish: ranch salad dressing

Place carrots in a plastic zipping bag.
Sprinkle with 3 tablespoons oil and
seasonings; toss to coat. Drizzle
remaining oil over a baking sheet; place
carrots in a single layer on sheet. Bake,
uncovered, at 425 degrees for 25 to
35 minutes, until carrots are golden.
Serve with salad dressing for dipping.
Makes 4 to 6 servings.

Kelly Gray
Weston, WV

My children didn't know until
they were almost grown that
this dish was good for them!
The sweet flavor mixed with
the spicy seasonings is
unusual and delicious.

BBQ Beef & Wagon Wheels Salad

2 c. cooked wagon wheel pasta
1 c. deli roast beef, cut in thin
   strips
3/4 c. onion, sliced
1/2 c. green pepper, chopped
2/3 c. barbecue sauce
2 T. Dijon mustard
2 c. red leaf lettuce, torn
2 c. green leaf lettuce, torn
Garnish: 1 tomato, sliced

Rinse pasta with cold water; drain well. Combine pasta, beef, onion and green pepper in a medium bowl; set aside. In a small bowl, mix together barbecue sauce and mustard; stir into beef mixture. Chill. At serving time, toss together red and green lettuce; arrange on salad plates. Spoon beef mixture over lettuce; garnish with tomato slices. Serves 4.

77

Vickie

A hearty salad for cowboy-size appetites.

French Onion Biscuits

8-oz. container French onion dip
1/4 c. milk
1 t. dried parsley
2 c. biscuit baking mix
1 T. butter, melted

In a large bowl, whisk together onion dip, milk and parsley until smooth. Stir in baking mix until well blended. Drop dough by spoonfuls onto a lightly greased baking sheet, making 12 biscuits. Bake at 450 degrees for 7 to 8 minutes, until lightly golden. Immediately brush tops of biscuits with melted butter. Makes one dozen.

Lane Ann Miller
Trenton, KY

These biscuits are quick, easy and scrumptious...wonderful with soups or Italian dishes.

Company Green Beans

3 slices bacon, crisply cooked, crumbled and 1 T. drippings reserved
2 t. garlic, minced
1/4 c. red onion, finely grated
2 14-1/2 oz. cans French-style green beans, drained
1 tomato, chopped
salt and pepper to taste
1/2 c. shredded sharp Cheddar cheese

79

In a skillet over medium heat, sauté garlic and onion in reserved bacon drippings until slightly softened. Remove from heat and stir in green beans, tomato and seasonings to taste. Place in a greased 8"x8" baking pan and sprinkle with cheese. Bake, covered, at 400 degrees for 15 minutes. Uncover, reduce heat to 350 degrees and bake an additional 15 minutes. Serves 4 to 6.

Stephanie Norton
Saginaw, TX

My husband's family has been sharing this dish at gatherings for generations. It's a staple at our house as well, even for those who don't like vegetables!

Chili Rice

3 c. cooked rice
10-3/4 oz. can cream of celery
    soup
4-oz. can diced green chiles,
    or to taste
1 c. shredded Monterey Jack cheese
1 c. sour cream
Optional: dried chives

Combine all ingredients except chives.
Transfer to a lightly greased 2-quart
casserole dish. Bake, uncovered, at
350 degrees for 20 minutes. Garnish
with chives, if desired. Serves 6 to 8.

Sally Davison
Page, AZ

People love this
five-ingredient casserole!
It goes well with other
southwestern dishes.

Black-Eyed Pea Salad

1/3 c. onion, grated
1/3 c. fresh parsley, minced
3 T. cider vinegar
2 T. oil
1 clove garlic, minced
1/4 t. salt
2 16-oz. cans black-eyed peas,
  drained
1 tomato, diced
1 head lettuce, shredded
Garnish: tomato wedges,
  green pepper rings

Combine onion, parsley, vinegar, oil, garlic and salt in a large bowl. Add peas and tomato; chill. At serving time, arrange lettuce on a platter. Spoon mixture over lettuce. Garnish with tomato wedges and green pepper rings. Serves 6 to 8.

Annette Sykes
Springfield, TN
My friends & family always ask me to bring this unique salad to potluck suppers.

Sweet-and-Sour Slaw

3-oz. pkg. chicken-flavored
   ramen noodles, uncooked
16-oz. pkg. shredded coleslaw mix
1 c. slivered almonds
1 c. sunflower kernels
4 green onions, chopped
6-oz. pkg. grilled chicken breast
   strips
11-oz. can mandarin oranges,
   drained

Break ramen noodles into pieces; set aside seasoning packet for dressing. In a large bowl, toss noodles with remaining ingredients. Drizzle with Dressing; toss again. Cover and refrigerate for at least one hour. Toss again before serving. Serves 6.

Dressing:

1/4 to 1/2 c. olive oil
1/4 c. sugar
3 T. white vinegar
reserved seasoning packet

Whisk together all ingredients.

Vicki Sebring
Mentor, OH

A different take on coleslaw that could be a meal in itself!

Hawaiian Asparagus

1 lb. asparagus, trimmed and cut
    in 1-inch diagonal slices
2 T. olive oil
1/4 c. beef broth
4 to 5 slices bacon, crisply
    cooked and cut into bite-size
    pieces
pepper to taste
2 T. sesame seed, lightly toasted

In a skillet over medium heat, cook
asparagus in oil for 2 to 3 minutes.
Add beef broth; cover, reduce heat
and simmer for 4 to 5 minutes,
until asparagus is cooked to desired
tenderness. Stir in bacon, pepper
and sesame seed. Serves 4.

83

Beth Brown
Trent Woods, NC

This recipe was given to
my mom forty years ago by
another military wife when
my Air Force family was
stationed in Japan. We make
this when asparagus is
in season.

Mustard-Topped Cauliflower

1 head cauliflower, cut into
  flowerets
1/3 c. water
1/2 c. mayonnaise
1 T. onion, finely chopped
2 t. mustard
1/4 t. salt
2/3 c. shredded Cheddar cheese
1/4 t. paprika

Place cauliflower in a deep microwave-safe casserole dish; add water. Cover and microwave on high for about 12 minutes, or until cauliflower is tender; drain. In a bowl, combine mayonnaise, onion, mustard and salt. Spoon mayonnaise mixture over cauliflower; sprinkle with cheese and paprika. Microwave, uncovered, for 2 minutes, or until cheese is melted. Serves 4 to 6.

Sandra Moy
Clarendon, NY

This recipe is amazing.
It takes only a few minutes
and you have a hearty side
dish that goes so well
with baked ham.

Baked Spinach & Rice

10-oz. pkg. frozen chopped
   spinach, thawed and well
   drained
2 c. cooked rice
8-oz. pkg. pasteurized process
   cheese spread, cubed
1/3 c. onion, chopped
1/3 c. red pepper, chopped
3 eggs, beaten
1/8 t. pepper
Optional: 1/4 lb. turkey bacon,
   crisply cooked and crumbled

In a large bowl, combine all
ingredients, mixing well. Spread in
a greased 10"x6" baking pan; smooth
top with a spatula. Bake, uncovered,
at 350 degrees for 30 minutes. Let
stand 5 minutes; cut into squares.
Makes 8 servings.

85

Elena Smith
Monterey, CA
I find this casserole is just
as tasty if I substitute
four egg whites for the
whole eggs and use a
"light" cheese spread.

Slow-Cooker Potatoes Dijonnaise

1/3 c. Dijon mustard
1/2 c. olive oil
1/3 c. red wine vinegar
salt and pepper to taste
6 potatoes, cubed
1 onion, chopped

Blend mustard, oil and vinegar in a medium bowl; add salt and pepper to taste. Add potatoes and onion, stirring to coat. Transfer to a slow cooker; cover and cook on low setting for 8 to 10 hours, until potatoes are tender. Makes 4 to 5 servings.

Dawn Dhooghe
Concord, NC
The house smells heavenly while this is cooking!

Garden Rice Salad

2 c. long-cooking brown rice,
   uncooked
1 carrot, peeled and sliced
1/2 cucumber, chopped
1/2 onion, chopped
1 green pepper, chopped
8 radishes, sliced
2 stalks celery, sliced
11-oz. can corn, drained and
   rinsed

Cook rice according to package instructions; fluff with a fork and let cool. In a bowl, combine rice and remaining ingredients. Drizzle with Dijon Dressing and toss to coat. Serves 4.

Dijon Dressing:
2 T. white vinegar
1 T. olive oil
1/4 c. lemon juice
2 T. Dijon mustard
salt and pepper to taste

Whisk together all ingredients in order listed.

87

Lori Peterson
Effingham, KS
Serve this deliciously different salad in a clear glass bowl to show off all the colors!

Orange-Filled Napoleons

8-oz. pkg. frozen puff pastry
   sheets, thawed
2 c. vanilla ice cream, softened
1 orange, peeled and thinly sliced
Garnish: powdered sugar

Unfold pastry and cut into 8 rectangles.
Place on an ungreased baking sheet and
bake at 375 degrees for 20 minutes, or
until puffed and golden. Let cool. To
serve, split pastries lengthwise. Spoon
ice cream on one half; top evenly with
orange slices and replace pastry top.
Dust with powdered sugar. Makes
4 servings.

Vickie

A snap to make and
elegant to serve!

Strawberry Dessert

16-1/2 oz. tube refrigerated sugar
cookie dough
8-oz. pkg. cream cheese,
softened
8-oz. container frozen whipped
topping, thawed and divided
1 qt. strawberries, hulled and
sliced
13-1/2 oz. container strawberry
glaze

Slice cookie dough and press
into the bottom of an ungreased
13"x9" baking pan. Bake at
350 degrees for 13 to 16 minutes,
until lightly golden. Cool completely
on a wire rack. Mix cream cheese
and one cup whipped topping.
Spread over cookie crust. Stir
strawberries and glaze together and
spread over top. Cover and chill.
Cut into squares and serve with
remaining whipped topping. Serves
10 to 12.

89

Janice Nichols
North Manchester, IN
A lady where I worked would
surprise the department with
this delicious dessert.
The sight of those fresh,
red strawberries would make
your mouth water!

Joyce's Chocolate Chip Pie

2 eggs, beaten
1/4 c. all-purpose flour
1/3 c. sugar
1-1/2 c. brown sugar, packed
1 c. chopped pecans
1/2 c. butter, melted and cooled
   slightly
3/4 c. mini semi-sweet chocolate
   chips
9-inch pie crust
Optional: whipped cream,
   additional mini chocolate chips

In a bowl, mix eggs, flour, sugars,
pecans and melted butter until well
blended. Sprinkle chocolate chips in
unbaked pie crust. Pour egg mixture
over top. Bake at 350 degrees for
30 minutes, or until golden. Pie will
become firm as it cools. Garnish as
desired. Serves 8.

Joyce Timko
Granite City, IL
Chocolate, butter and
whipped cream...oh, my!

Bananas Foster

1/2 c. butter, melted
1/4 c. brown sugar, packed
6 bananas, cut into 1-inch slices
1/4 c. rum or 1/4 t. rum extract
Garnish: vanilla ice cream

Stir together butter, brown sugar, bananas and rum or extract in a slow cooker. Cover and cook on low setting for one hour. Use a slotted spoon to place bananas into serving dishes. Top with a scoop of ice cream and drizzle with sauce from the slow cooker. Makes 4 servings.

91

Jo Ann
Guests will flip over this decadent slow-cooker dessert!

Peanut Butter Surprise Cookies

16-1/2 oz. tube refrigerated peanut
   butter cookie dough
12 mini peanut butter cups
1/3 c. semi-sweet chocolate chips
1 t. shortening

Divide cookie dough into 12 pieces.
With floured fingers, wrap one piece of
dough around each peanut butter cup.
Place on ungreased baking sheets. Bake
at 350 degrees for 10 to 15 minutes,
until golden. Cool on baking sheets
one minute; remove to wire rack to
cool completely. In a saucepan, melt
chocolate chips and shortening over
low heat, stirring constantly. Drizzle
melted chocolate over cookies. Let
stand until set. Makes one dozen.

Sherry Gordon
Arlington Heights, IL

Yum, yum, yum! I like to
divvy up the dough between
baking sheets and chill
the second batch while the
first is baking.

Chocolate-Berry Trifles

1 pt. blueberries, divided
1 pt. strawberries, hulled and
    sliced
1 angel food cake, cubed
1 c. chocolate syrup
12-oz. container frozen whipped
    topping, thawed

In a bowl, crush 1/4 cup blueberries.
Stir in remaining blueberries and
strawberries. Place several cake cubes
in the bottom of 10 clear serving
cups or bowls. Top with a layer of
berry mixture. Drizzle lightly with
chocolate syrup, then top with a
layer of whipped topping. Repeat
layers until each cup is full, ending
with a layer of whipped topping and
a light drizzle of chocolate syrup.
Makes 10 servings.

93

**Melody Taynor
Everett, WA**

I've made all kinds of
trifles, but this is my
first one with chocolate.
My sister says it's
my best yet!

Quick & Easy Nutty Cheese Bars

18-1/2 oz. pkg. golden butter
  cake mix
1-1/2 c. chopped pecans or
  walnuts, divided
3/4 c. butter, melted
2 8-oz. pkgs. cream cheese,
  softened
1 c. brown sugar, packed

In a bowl, combine dry cake mix,
3/4 cup pecans and melted butter; stir
until well blended. Press mixture into
the bottom of a greased 13"x9" baking
pan. Combine cream cheese and brown
sugar in a separate bowl. Stir until well
mixed. Spread evenly over crust.
Sprinkle with remaining pecans. Bake
at 350 degrees for 25 to 30 minutes,
until edges are golden and cheese
topping is set. Cool completely in pan
on wire rack. Cut into bars. Refrigerate
leftovers. Makes 2 dozen.

Donnie Carter
Wellington, TX
This recipe is now the
requested birthday gift of
family & friends. They're
so good cold!

Apple Crisp Pie

21-oz. can apple pie filling
9-inch deep-dish pie crust
1/2 c. brown sugar, packed
1/2 c. sugar
1 c. quick-cooking oats,
   uncooked
1 T. cinnamon
1/4 c. butter, sliced

Pour apple pie filling into pie crust.
In a separate bowl, combine sugars,
oats and cinnamon. Sprinkle over
top; dot with butter. Bake at
375 degrees for 30 minutes.
Serves 8.

95

Cris Hamilton
Anna, TX

My sister-in-law made this
for us one Easter. I can't
believe how easy and
delicious it is!

Mariachi Margarita Dip

8-oz. pkg. cream cheese, softened
1/3 c. frozen margarita drink mix,
   thawed
2 T. orange juice
1/4 c. powdered sugar
1/2 c. whipped cream
Garnish: corn syrup, colored sugar
assorted fruit slices and cubes

In a bowl, beat together cream cheese,
margarita mix, orange juice and
powdered sugar until smooth. Fold
whipped cream into mixture until well
blended. Cover and chill one hour.
Dip rim of serving bowl in corn syrup.
Shake off excess and dip rim in colored
sugar. Spoon dip into bowl and serve
with fruit. Serves 6 to 8.

Lynda Robson
Boston, MA

Turn any gathering into a
fiesta when you serve this
appetizer-style dessert!

Mom's Chocolate Malt Shoppe Pie

1-oz. pkg. sugar-free white
   chocolate instant pudding mix
4 to 5 t. chocolate malt powder
1 c. milk
8-oz. container frozen whipped
   topping, thawed and divided
1-1/2 c. malted milk balls,
   crushed and divided
9-inch chocolate cookie crust

In a bowl, mix together dry pudding
mix, malt powder and milk. Fold in
3/4 of the whipped topping and
1-1/4 cups crushed candy; spread
in crust. Spread with remaining
whipped topping. Sprinkle with
remaining candy; chill until set.
Serves 8.

97

Nancy Brush
Robinson, IL

We're a family of chocoholics
and also love chocolate
malts, so my mom created this
pie that combines our two
favorite things.

Root Beer Float Cake

18-1/2 oz. pkg. white cake mix
2-1/4 c. root beer, chilled and
   divided
1/4 c. oil
2 eggs, beaten
1 env. whipped topping mix

In a large bowl, combine dry cake mix,
1-1/4 cups root beer, oil and eggs; beat
until well blended. Pour into a greased
13"x9" baking pan. Bake at 350 degrees
for 30 to 35 minutes; cool completely.
In a medium bowl, with an electric
mixer on high speed, beat whipped
topping mix and remaining root beer
until soft peaks form; frost cake. Makes
24 servings.

Mary Patenaude
Griswold, CT

This cake is so easy
to make. And it tastes
just like a root beer float!

Coconut Cupcakes

99

2/3 c. sweetened flaked coconut
1-1/4 c. powdered sugar
1-1/2 c. all-purpose flour
1/8 t. salt
1 t. baking powder
1/2 c. butter, melted and cooled
   slightly
5 egg whites, beaten
12 raspberries

In a bowl, combine coconut, powdered sugar, flour, salt and baking powder. Mix in melted butter. Stir in egg whites until well combined. Line a muffin tin with 12 paper liners; fill liners with batter 2/3 full. Bake at 375 degrees for 12 to 15 minutes, until firm. Let cool. Spread Vanilla Frosting onto cupcakes; top each with a raspberry and let set. Makes one dozen.

Vanilla Frosting:

1-1/2 c. powdered sugar
1 t. vanilla extract
4 to 5 t. hot water

In a bowl, combine all ingredients. Beat to desired consistency, adding more water or sugar as needed.

Barb Horton
Cincinnati, OH
Fresh raspberries are perfect little toppers for these wonderful cupcakes!

Mix-and-Go Chocolate Cookies

18-1/2 oz. pkg. chocolate cake mix
1/2 c. butter, softened
2 eggs, beaten
1 c. white chocolate chips

In a bowl, combine dry cake mix,
butter and eggs until smooth. Mix in
chocolate chips. Drop by tablespoonfuls
onto ungreased baking sheets. Bake at
350 degrees for 8 to 10 minutes. Let
cool on baking sheet for 5 minutes;
remove to wire rack to cool completely.
Makes about 2 dozen.

Rhonda Reeder
Ellicott City, MD

Just as decadent with
peanut butter or milk
chocolate chips!

Oh-So-Easy Fruit Tartlets

2 3.4-oz. pkgs. instant vanilla
   pudding mix
3-1/2 c. milk
2 t. lemon zest
2 4-oz. pkgs. mini graham
   cracker crusts
Garnish: sliced kiwi, peaches
   or strawberries, mandarin
   oranges, raspberries,
   blueberries
1/2 c. apple jelly, melted

101

Prepare pudding according to
package directions, using the milk.
Stir in lemon zest. Spoon into
mini crusts; arrange fruit on top as
desired. Use a pastry brush to glaze
fruit with melted jelly. Set tartlets
on a baking sheet, cover and chill.
Makes one dozen.

Jennifer Licon-Conner
Gooseberry Patch
Guests will be so impressed
with these bakery-style
tarts! Use your favorite
pudding flavor and fruit to
make different varieties.

Fudge Cobbler

1/2 c. butter
1-oz. sq. unsweetened baking
   chocolate
1 c. sugar
1/2 c. all-purpose flour
1 t. vanilla extract
2 eggs, beaten
Optional: vanilla ice cream

Melt butter and chocolate in a saucepan over low heat, stirring often. Remove from heat; stir in sugar, flour, vanilla and eggs. Pour batter into a greased 8"x8" baking pan; bake at 325 degrees for 20 to 22 minutes. Serve warm with ice cream, if desired. Serves 9.

Sandy Bernards
Valencia, CA

Mmm...so easy, so luscious.
What could be better?

White Chocolate-Butterscotch Pretzels

1 lb. white melting chocolate
15-oz. pkg. mini pretzels
1/2 c. butterscotch chips

Break up white chocolate into about 6 pieces and place in a microwave-safe dish. Microwave on high for 1-1/2 to 2 minutes, stirring every 30 seconds, until melted and smooth. Dip pretzels into the chocolate and lay on wax paper to dry. Melt butterscotch chips in the microwave repeating instructions for the chocolate. Spoon melted butterscotch into a plastic zipping bag; snip off a corner. Drizzle butterscotch over pretzels. Let pretzels set for a few hours, or overnight if packing into gift bags. Makes about 2 pounds.

103

Buffy VanSickle
Buhl, ID

Kids love to help with this simple-to-make treat! Perfect for Halloween treat bags or Christmas goodie trays.

Oh, Harry! Bars

3/4 c. butter, softened
1 c. dark brown sugar, packed
1/2 c. honey
1/2 t. ground ginger
4 c. quick-cooking oats, uncooked
6-oz. pkg. milk chocolate chips
2/3 c. creamy peanut butter

In a bowl, beat butter and brown sugar until light and fluffy. Beat in honey and ginger; stir in oats. With moistened hands, pat mixture into the bottom of a greased 13"x9" baking pan. Bake at 350 degrees until bubbly and lightly golden, about 25 minutes. In a microwave-safe bowl, heat chocolate chips and peanut butter on high for one minute. Stir; heat for another minute. Stir until all chips are melted. Spread chocolate mixture over bars and refrigerate until set. Cut into bars. Makes 2 dozen.

Valarie Lewis
Clifford Township, PA
My mother handed down this dessert recipe to me. Growing up, it was a favorite among us kids!

Little Cheesecakes

1 c. graham cracker crumbs
1 c. sugar, divided
1/4 c. butter, melted
2 8-oz. pkgs. cream cheese,
    softened
2 eggs, beaten
1 t. vanilla extract
14-1/2 oz. can cherry pie filling

Place mini paper liners into 24 mini muffin cups. In a bowl, combine cracker crumbs, 1/4 cup sugar and butter. Press about 2 teaspoons of mixture into the bottom of each liner. In a bowl, beat cream cheese and remaining sugar together. Add eggs and vanilla; mix well. Evenly spoon cheese mixture over crusts. Bake at 350 degrees for 15 minutes, or until set. Cool. Top with cherry pie filling. Makes 2 dozen.

105

Nina Jones
Springfield, OH

I started making this recipe when I was a teenager...now it's a favorite of my teenage son and his friends.

Easy Apple Popovers

10-oz. tube refrigerated flaky
  biscuits
2 c. sweetened applesauce
1 c. powdered sugar
3 to 4 T. milk

Spray a muffin tin with non-stick
vegetable spray. Separate biscuits.
Press a biscuit into the bottom and
partway up the sides of each muffin
cup. Spoon applesauce into biscuits.
Bake at 300 degrees for about 10 to
15 minutes, until biscuits are done.
Remove popovers from muffin tin; let
cool. Mix powdered sugar and milk to
a drizzling consistency; drizzle over
popovers. Makes 10 servings.

Debra Coogle
Oglethorpe, GA

These fruity treats are
delish! I made up this recipe
when I needed a dessert to
carry to the family of a
friend who had just come
home from the hospital.

Raspberry Cheese Ball

2 8-oz pkgs. cream cheese,
   softened
1/4 c. raspberry preserves
2 c. pecans, finely chopped and
   divided
assorted cookies and crackers

In a bowl, beat cream cheese until creamy; mix in preserves and one cup pecans. Shape into a ball and roll in remaining pecans. Serve with cookies and crackers. Serves 6 to 8.

107

Julie Ann Perkins
Anderson, IN

Try different preserves to accommodate everyone's tastes...cherry, apricot or even boysenberry!

INDEX

Beverages

Good Morning Blueberry Shake, 20
Kitchen Café Mocha, 13

Breads

Coconut-Orange Breakfast Rolls, 8
Easiest Cinnamon-Raisin Rolls, 21
French Onion Biscuits, 78
Nutty Brown Sugar Muffins, 10
Pamela's Garlic Bread, 72
Sour Cream Cornbread, 74

Breakfast

Apple-Stuffed French Toast, 12
Breakfast Bruschetta, 17
Buttermilk Oven Pancakes, 16
Butterscotch Coffee Cake, 22
Cream Cheesy Strudel, 26
Egg & Bacon Quesadillas, 7
Ham & Feta Cheese Omelet, 19
Make-Ahead Cheese & Egg Casserole, 27
Savory Breakfast Pancakes, 9
Scott's Wonderful Waffles, 23
Slow-Cooker Hashbrown Casserole, 18
Sunrise Pizza, 11
Sweet & Spicy Bacon, 25
Trail Mix Bagels, 24

Condiments

No-Cook Strawberry Freezer Jam, 15
Peachy Waffle Topping, 14

Cookies

Mix-and-Go Chocolate Cookies, 100
Oh, Harry! Bars, 104
Peanut Butter Surprise Cookies, 92
Quick & Easy Nutty Cheese Bars, 94

Desserts

Apple Crisp Pie, 95
Bananas Foster, 91
Chocolate-Berry Trifles, 93
Coconut Cupcakes, 99
Easy Apple Popovers, 106
Fudge Cobbler, 102
Joyce's Chocolate Chip Pie, 90
Little Cheesecakes, 105
Mariachi Margarita Dip, 96
Mom's Chocolate Malt Shoppe Pie, 97
Oh-So-Easy Fruit Tartlets, 101
Orange-Filled Napoleons, 88
Raspberry Cheese Ball, 107
Root Beer Float Cake, 98
Strawberry Dessert, 89
White Chocolate-Butterscotch Pretzels, 103

Mains

Apple-Stuffed Turkey Breast, 46
Apricot-Glazed Ham Steaks, 58
Baked Pork Medallions, 60
Balsamic Chicken & Pears, 28
Beef & Potato Roll, 55
Cheesy Ham & Vegetable Bake, 53
Chicken & Peppers Stir-Fry, 45

INDEX

Company's Coming Pork Chops, 34
Creamy Chicken Bake, 48
Dill Rice & Chicken, 57
Down-Home Taco Casserole, 59
Easy Skillet Lasagna, 35
Easy Sweet-and-Sour Chicken, 56
Foil-Wrapped Baked Salmon, 54
Honey Cornmeal Chicken, 67
Italian Sausage Skillet, 29
Jambalaya in a Jiff, 31
Jax's Cheeseburger Pizzas, 63
Lemony "Baked" Chicken, 42
Little Meatloaves, 62
Mandy's Hand-Battered Chicken, 41
Mexicana Veggie Bake, 64
Parmesan Baked Chicken, 52
Patsy's Stuffed Pork Chops, 65
Penne & Spring Vegetables, 44
Poor Man's Steak & Vegetables, 50
Salmon Cornbread Cakes, 36
Skillet Dinner, 40
Speedy Steak & Veggies, 61
Spicy Salsa Twists, 39
Sunday Meatball Skillet, 43
Zippy Broiled Catfish, 51

Salads

BBQ Beef & Wagon Wheels Salad, 77
Black-Eyed Pea Salad, 81
Garden Rice Salad, 87
Raspberry Spinach Salad, 71
Sweet-and-Sour Slaw, 82
Tangy Watermelon Salad, 69

Sandwiches

Asian Chicken Wraps, 30
Hearty Chicken-Bacon Melts, 47
Key West Burgers, 32
Potluck Beef Sandwiches, 66
Saucy Slow-Cooker Pulled Pork, 38

Sides

Baked Spinach & Rice, 85
Chili Rice, 80
Company Green Beans, 79
Corn Surprise, 68
Fried Spaghetti, 73
Hawaiian Asparagus, 83
Mustard-Topped Cauliflower, 84
Ripe Tomato Tart, 70
Slow-Cooker Potatoes Dijonnaise, 86
Spiced Baked Fruit, 75
Spicy Carrot French Fries, 76

Soups

Chili & Biscuits, 49
Hug in a Mug Soup, 37
Unstuffed Green Pepper Soup, 33

Tangy Watermelon Salad, page 69

Mustard-Topped Cauliflower, page 84

Coconut Cupcakes, page 99

Patsy's Stuffed Pork Chops, page 65

Our Story

Back in 1984, we were next-door neighbors raising our families in the little town of Delaware, Ohio. Two moms with small children, we were looking for a way to do what we loved and stay home with the kids too. We had always shared a love of home cooking and making memories with family & friends and so, after many a conversation over the backyard fence, **Gooseberry Patch** was born.

We put together our first catalog at our kitchen tables, enlisting the help of our loved ones wherever we could. From that very first mailing, we found an immediate connection with many of our customers and it wasn't long before we began receiving letters, photos and recipes from these new friends. In 1992, we put together our very first cookbook, compiled from hundreds of these recipes and, the rest, as they say, is history.

Hard to believe it's been over 25 years since those kitchen-table days! From that original little **Gooseberry Patch** family, we've grown to include an amazing group of creative folks who love cooking, decorating and creating as much as we do. Today, we're best known for our homestyle, family-friendly cookbooks, now recognized as national bestsellers.

Jo Ann & Vickie

One thing's for sure, we couldn't have done it without our friends all across the country. Each year, we're honored to turn thousands of your recipes into our collectible cookbooks. Our hope is that each book captures the stories and heart of all of you who have shared with us. Whether you've been with us since the beginning or are just discovering us, welcome to the **Gooseberry Patch** family!

Visit us online:
www.gooseberrypatch.com
1·800·854·6673

U.S. to Canadian Recipe Equivalents

Volume Measurements

1/4 teaspoon	1 mL
1/2 teaspoon	2 mL
1 teaspoon	5 mL
1 tablespoon = 3 teaspoons	15 mL
2 tablespoons = 1 fluid ounce	30 mL
1/4 cup	60 mL
1/3 cup	75 mL
1/2 cup = 4 fluid ounces	125 mL
1 cup = 8 fluid ounces	250 mL
2 cups = 1 pint =16 fluid ounces	500 mL
4 cups = 1 quart	1 L

Weights

1 ounce	30 g
4 ounces	120 g
8 ounces	225 g
16 ounces = 1 pound	450 g

Oven Temperatures

300° F	150° C
325° F	160° C
350° F	180° C
375° F	190° C
400° F	200° C
450° F	230° C

Baking Pan Sizes

Square

8x8x2 inches	2 L = 20x20x5 cm
9x9x2 inches	2.5 L = 23x23x5 cm

Rectangular

13x9x2 inches	3.5 L = 33x23x5 cm

Loaf

9x5x3 inches	2 L = 23x13x7 cm

Round

8x1-1/2 inches	1.2 L = 20x4 cm
9x1-1/2 inches	1.5 L = 23x4 cm

Recipe Abbreviations

t. = teaspoon	ltr. = liter
T. = tablespoon	oz. = ounce
c. = cup	lb. = pound
pt. = pint	doz. = dozen
qt. = quart	pkg. = package
gal. = gallon	env. = envelope

Kitchen Measurements

A pinch = 1/8 tablespoon	1 fluid ounce = 2 tablespoons
3 teaspoons = 1 tablespoon	4 fluid ounces = 1/2 cup
2 tablespoons = 1/8 cup	8 fluid ounces = 1 cup
4 tablespoons = 1/4 cup	16 fluid ounces = 1 pint
8 tablespoons = 1/2 cup	32 fluid ounces = 1 quart
16 tablespoons = 1 cup	16 ounces net weight = 1 pound
2 cups = 1 pint	
4 cups = 1 quart	
4 quarts = 1 gallon	